Dedication

Late-night writings
Humming sound of the refrigerator
A timely and calm sleeping daughter
My wife, parents, and friends for never doubting me
And all those who love nature, science, and relationships

Who this book is for:

For the man who genuinely wishes to help his spouse during all phases of pregnancy.

For the couple planning to have a baby sometime soon.

For the woman who wants her spouse to be more involved in her pregnancy.

For men who do not know that a pregnancy is much more than a woman carrying a baby for nine months.

For women who wish to know how a pregnancy affects men.

For curious readers who love nature, science, and relationships.

What this book is not:

This is not a standard guide on what medically happens during nine months of pregnancy.

This book does not deal with advance topics like adopting a baby or medically induced pregnancy methods or dealing with food allergies or some complex medical condition in a pregnancy.

Contents

Disclaimer

THE INFORMATION PROVIDED IN THIS book is designed to provide helpful information on the subjects discussed. This book is not meant to be used, nor should it be used, to diagnose or treat any medical condition. For diagnosis or treatment of any medical problem, consult your own physician. The publisher and author are not responsible for any specific health or allergy needs that may require medical supervision and are not liable for any damages or negative consequences from any treatment, action, application, or preparation to any person reading or following the information in this book.

While best efforts have been used in preparing this book, the author and publisher make no representations or warranties of any kind and assume no liabilities of any kind with respect to the accuracy or completeness of the contents. Neither the author nor the publisher shall be held liable or responsible to any person or entity with respect to any loss or incidental or consequential damages caused, or alleged to have been caused, directly or indirectly, by the information contained herein.

References are provided for informational purposes only and do not constitute endorsement of any websites or other sources. Readers should be aware that the websites listed in this book may change their content.

About the Author

BORN AND BROUGHT UP IN India, I am the first engineer in a family of doctors and lawyers. After studying computer science and getting a master's degree from the University of Southern California, I have been working in the field of Internet advertising and computer software development. Most important, I am the father of a four-year-old daughter named Urja. (Urja in Sanskrit means energy. She is definitely a bundle of joy, very curious in nature, and now the master of surprising her parents with her witty comments.)

I was the first in my circle of friends to become a father. I was twenty-eight at that time, and having been away from my parents for school and work for so long, it was hard to learn all the new things I needed to know about pregnancy. I was completely clueless about what pregnancy really means. My wife and I planned our pregnancy in advance, and we did everything right, but we still had to go through a lot of self-realization and read a lot. My wife, Priya, approached her pregnancy in a very positive way and stayed on top of pregnancy-related issues. She was always on the lookout for new information and always shared any new information she found with me. For that I am very thankful to her. Without her amazing understanding, I would have surely felt much more overwhelmed.

When her friends started getting pregnant, they began asking for suggestions and recommendations for their own pregnancy-related questions. My wife and her friends kept asking me to write down important things about pregnancy that we'd learned, and they specifically wanted something to help their husbands feel more involved in their pregnancies.

First I tried to find books to help them, but all I could find were books with lots of medical information about pregnancy, and most were geared toward women. Some books detailed food intake down to the ounce, and some books literally frightened men by telling them how much a pregnancy would suck out of their lives. Surprisingly, there were not many books geared toward men to help them understand pregnancy in a positive, balanced way. So I decided to compile my thought process in a structured way in this book, to help others learn, and to help them plan a better pregnancy by having the right attitude toward it.

The statistics or medical or scientific terminologies used in this book have mostly been compiled and verified from Internet resources such as Wikipedia.com, BabyCenter.com, and WebMD.com, to name a few.

Though this is a small book, instead of putting you readers right into details of pregnancy I will start it slow with first two chapters with some background. I hope you learn a lot as you read more and more, that it helps you prepare for, understand, and go through the journey of pregnancy with a positive attitude.

Special thanks to three lovely ladies of my life—my mother, my wife and daughter—for their unconditional love, support and encouragements to me and my projects.

I wish you all the best with your own journey into pregnancy and beyond!

Best wishes,
Pratik Patil

pratikspace@gmail.com
Twitter: @pratikspace
#pregnancyandmen

CHAPTER 1

What is Pregnancy?

Let's start with the literal meaning of the word
pregnancy:
Pregnancy |ˈpregnənsē|
noun (pl. -cies)
Period of being pregnant

IS IT JUST FOR NINE months? Or is that what it really means? Does it have a deeper meaning? Where does it all really start? Why do we really need to get pregnant? Why does it need a sperm and an egg?

Questions are many, but they all come down to the two most basic and natural aspects of life that have been engineered in the genetic makeup of every living being on earth: *survival* and *reproduction.*

Ultimately survival and reproduction are linked to each other—to survive and to have any potential chance for reproduction, or to be able to reproduce to survive, is nature's meaning of life.

Every single species wants to survive against all odds, but with the blessing of our advanced brain capabilities, we humans try to survive in a much better way than everyone else. That gives our bodies, and eventually our minds, greater reproductive success in bringing our offspring into this world, where they have a better chance of survival and ultimately reproduce and carry on.

But why has nature given us this entirely hardwired physical urge to reproduce, and what is its real purpose in the grand equation of the cosmos? That is something that goes into spiritual and celestial nature, and I will leave it up to each reader to come up with his or her own version of the truth.

In my perspective nature has ingrained us with its own curious and experimental qualities. To realize the full potential of those, nature needs this cycle of reproductions with small variations each time, fine tuning its process, that would one day leads us to become a much greater species, realizing our true purpose and ultimately feeding back into nature to make it grow.

But if all nature expects from us is to reproduce, then why can't we reproduce in the simplest way like a cell dividing into two, then quadrupling, and so on, as in full person to person cloning? Why start with a baby? Why start with a meeting of sperm and egg?

The answer is because, otherwise, such product will never get an immunity to face against any non-native change, because that does not improve in its physical and mental capabilities as cycles go on. And if something does not survive better in the test of time, then nature does not want it and eventually nature will get rid of it and start another experiment of its own.

Nature is a self-improving cosmic machine, and it has found a perfect balance over its billions of years of experimenting by bringing together two completely opposite genetic sets that share a common hope of harboring a better life; and that's the genesis of a pregnancy!

CHAPTER 2

Nature Versus Nurture

IF YOU ARE JUST GOING with the flow, you might find yourself lost into this intricate maze of the pregnancy. Before we dive deep into pregnancy and related issues, we need to know what is the formula of success. When time will come to measure the success of a pregnancy, you can think of a number of aspects, but in the end there are only two dimensions to this success: *nature* and *nurture.*

NATURE

Nature deals with genetics on a biochemical level. It's what you eat, and the quality and quantity of certain chemicals, vitamins, and minerals in your body. It deals with so many physical and biological things that it's automatic. You cannot really control nature; it's engineered as part of your genes, and your genes know what to do and when to do it.

NURTURE

Nurture goes to the metaphysical level. It's abstract. It deals with *how* rather than *what.* The essence of the metaphysics is in the nature of one's mind. It deals with how you do things, how consciously you make an effort to do something, and how you handle situations.

When you discuss pregnancy with people who had a normal, happy pregnancy and a healthy child, you realize that nature and nurture are not on opposite sides. They have to go together, hand in hand, in perfect balance. If you strive for that, you do not need to worry about the end result because it will turn out to be a pretty good one.

When you are working toward a better pregnancy, set some goals. You have to dedicate your time and commit to these efforts.

DEDICATION

You are probably a very busy person with lots of things going on in your life. Maybe it's because of your profession, your hobbies, your extracurricular activities, or your family, and at the end of the day, you get very tired. Remember, things will always be busy, but you have to dedicate some time for yourself for this. There are some important things and a lot of not-so-important things in a day. Try to sort these out and plan some time for your own self-improvement. Set aside some time to spend with your family. It's not only beneficial for pregnancy—such dedication will definitely make you a better individual and a better parent.

COMMITMENT

Deciding to dedicate time for doing things is one thing, but following through consistently is totally another. Commitment is important. From my personal experience, I realized that somehow my plans to go to the gym never stay consistent beyond two weeks. Something happens and I stop going. For things like this, you have to remember why you are making these special efforts: as part of planning a better pregnancy. It's ultimately you—the future parent—and your child who will benefit from your planning. For a better cause, you will push yourself to stretch your own physical and mental limits.

Commitment does not come from just doing regular exercise; it also comes from taking control of your body. Addiction to something is bad. If you are a smoker or regular alcohol drinker, then for the betterment of your own health and for better health for your future kids, please stop, or control your urges as much as you can at least a month or two before you plan to conceive. It's like having a fishing ban in seas where the number of fish has been depleted. If you give enough time for nature to recover, their numbers grow again. Your health, especially your sperm's health, will definitely flourish if you can control those bad health addictions.

Smoking and drinking are not the only addictions, these days, in the world of 140-character blogs, six-second videos, cryptic text abbreviations, disappearing messages, ever-growing friend feeds, and never-ending breaking news, you have to remember when to stop! Just reading about what you do on your gadgets can be overwhelming; imagine what's going through your brain when you keep doing it again and again.

Your electronic toys need to be put on hold. They will keep buzzing unless you keep those fun apps on silent settings. Stop counting how many likes you are getting or how many likes other people are getting or how awesome someone's pictures are and how your pictures never come out good. Stop comparing your life with everything on the Internet. Some things are just not worth it. Internet addiction is a bad thing. Most people think it's harmless to keep track of all this, but it's an addiction. It makes you feel different, for better or worse, and it unknowingly takes away a lot of time from the limited daily hours you have. *The greatest investment you can do in your life is in gaining time.* If you can control it, you will have more time and you might feel more focused on the other important things—like pregnancy —that you are trying to achieve.

Nature with nurture

The way your genes will interact and the way the development of a baby will happen can be left to nature, but you have to make sure to take care of all other worldly things for your wife.

Be conscious about the things that her doctor tells you about, check on her diet, ask her to keep a healthy diet, research some good exercises for her and suggest them. Drive more carefully when she is around. Make sure she is comfortable wherever she is. If she is a working professional, ask her to take breaks at work and take short walks. Ask her to read good books (if she likes to read), show her happy movies, spend time with her, invite her friends over, be in touch with future grandparents.

Every small but conscious effort will make things go smoothly and will lead to greater satisfaction.

Sometimes it happens that many couples do want to have a baby *some day* in their life but they never consciously plan for a pregnancy and turns out nature happens to find its way first. In those scenarios people just have to assume that whatever nature has done is in their best interests and concentrate on nurturing the pregnancy. But surely if you plan it better, you may not need a lot of nurturing efforts or worries later, that's why pre-planning is super important for men.

CHAPTER 3

Preplanning

A LOT OF MEN THINK that with the blessing of ever-regenerating sperm, all they need to do is impregnate their wives, and that is the only part for them to play in a pregnancy!

A lot of times women complain, *"Men have little to do beyond conception into a pregnancy"* As if no one cares what a man contributes, or how significant that contribution is. Most people think that the real trouble of pregnancy belongs to women. Though I do not deny that part, indeed they do go through most of it, but there is a big part we men play in pregnancy, and it's definitely not just getting a woman pregnant. A lot of men also blame the woman if something goes wrong with her pregnancy, but it could be the man's fault for not having, or not preparing for, healthy enough sperm!

In reality, getting a woman pregnant is a very small part of the childbirth equation. The strength and health of your sperm can cause everlasting affect your future kid's health, and every small improvement you make in your mind and body before pregnancy will matter then.

The health of your future kids does not start with their birth—it starts with you, right now, well before you plan to impregnate your wife.

If you do not care about your health in your current lifestyle, if you keep eating any kind of food regardless of its good or bad effects on your health, if you drink or smoke a lot and do not exercise, then do not expect to have positive health benefits, or a very long life to pass on to your future kids. If that's the case for you, and if you are thinking about pregnancy, it's not too late for you to fix your health, or at least to improve it.

It's not just your health that is important. Your wife needs to be healthy as well. If her lifestyle is not that healthy, you will have to talk about this with her. Gain her confidence and convince her to have a healthy lifestyle going forward. If you want a worry-free pregnancy and healthy childbirth, the healthier the better for both of you!

A part of preplanning involves asking both of you, as a couple, a few questions:

- Why do you want to have a baby?
- Is this the right time for you both, as a couple, to have a baby in your life?
- Are you ready to take good care of your newborn and take care of your own health?

If you are really not sure, then doing this just for the sake of doing it or just because someone else is doing it, may not produce good outcomes for you or your kid because you may not be in this situation for the right reasons.

So at least give it a thought. That's definitely a good start to being a better parent in the future.

There are a lot of couples who are extremely busy in their lives, and a lot of women prefer to work. It's better for a couple to talk about the big change in their future that they will experience together and to discuss the challenges of taking care of a newborn.

Remember, no one is ever really 100 percent ready to have a baby. But you will have to decide if it's the appropriate time in your life and go for it. After all, we humans are no different from any other animals. Humans have created money and professions for their own social and cultural and civilized reasons, but in the end, like all other species, we are genetically born to do two main things: survive and reproduce. So take your time, but someday you will have to think about it.

You do not need to have a million dollars in your bank account, but realize that a newborn will definitely add extra bucks to your household budget. As they grow older, these expenses add up more. So it's better to get a view of your current and future finances, and think about what you can comfortably manage and what you cannot, and if there are any ways you can improve it going forward.

If you are in the habit of regularly saving money, if you are not broke, if you have a basic financial cushion, then you can manage. Your baby planning can surely go ahead financially. You can always improve upon it as time goes by.

Any sort of help helps! You will have to think about ways of making your wife comfortable during and after her pregnancy. If you can, convince your wife's parents to come over and stay with her for a few weeks or months (whatever is manageable) during, and maybe even after, her pregnancy. It might help her feel more comfortable in her time of need. Bringing your own parents might not be the best-case scenario, unless of course your wife is genuinely comfortable staying with them, but keep them as a backup option.

Having good friends around where you live can make things more comfortable for both of you, especially in case of any urgent help you might need. During pregnancy, it's also better if you socialize with your close friends more so they will be inclined to help more and provide support. In social settings especially in the company of close friends you feel more relaxed, and that helps reduce the stress you might feel from pregnancy and related issues.

There is one more thing I would suggest for anyone planning a baby soon: Do your and your wife's full range of blood tests through a lab. This will give you a better idea of your current health and alert you if you have any major issues, like high cholesterol, blood pressure, thyroid problems, or any issues that were not previously diagnosed. This will definitely make your planning go more smoothly, and if any changes are needed they can be made early on.

This will help you to better plan your future with the right mind-set. Hopefully you are now over the thought that your work is limited to getting your wife pregnant.

CHAPTER 4

The Knowing

It's a common misunderstanding that nature has gifted men with unlimited sperm and that is enough for pregnancy.

Let's get straight to the point: for a healthy pregnancy, there is nothing more important than to keep your sperm healthy!

You do not need to know a lot of biological details about sperm, nor the medical terms for it, but just for a general understanding, apart from white-looking fluid that your low-hanging fruits produce, an individual sperm looks like a balloon attached to a string. Its head contains all your genetic material, while the tail acts like a propulsion system that pushes it deeper to find an egg inside a woman's body. Once it meets a spherical-looking egg, one sperm manages to penetrate it, and that gets your wife pregnant! Voilà!

Assuming that your wife's health is fine and her egg is ready, the health of your sperm decides how soon your wife can get pregnant. Weak health of sperm can take many tries, or even worse, weak sperm may not naturally get your wife pregnant—ever. But a healthy sperm can do wonders the first time you decide to not use any protection!

For the health of the sperm, how healthy you look from the outside does not matter. What matters is what you eat, how good your immune system is, and how you try to keep your body healthy. All those things affect the health of your sperm directly.

Weakness of sperm can be because a variety of problems:

- Low sperm count;
- Thickening of the liquid surrounding the sperm so there is less room to swim;
- Less oxygen in your blood stream, leading to less-active sperm;
- Sperm that is unable to travel the distance to find the egg, or even if found, lacking the energy to effectively penetrate it;
- And changes occurring due to your advancing age.

A little-known factor that can affect your sperm is your technology habits—yes, using your gadgets on your lap! Remember, heat is bad for your sperm. There is a reason why your low-hanging fruits are designed to stay outside your body: they need to stay cooler than your body; only in that way can they be functional in creating good sperm. Extra heat for extended time can degrade sperm's health as well as count. So a couple of things to avoid: no tight underwear—hello, boxers—keep them loose, no Jacuzzi and sauna time for you for a couple of weeks before conception, no keeping electronic gadgets on your lap for long periods of time, no extreme exercising that can heat up your body for a long time. Anything that could cause an increase in body temperature—especially in your private areas—for a long time, please avoid!

We will look into ways of avoiding weaknesses in following chapters as well, but here I specifically want to point out a very important factor: *age.*

Your age plays a very important role in your sperm's health. In your early twenties, your sperm will be much healthier than it will be after your mid-thirties. Like the rest of the body, sperm also starts to age, and it starts degrading as more and more years pass.

Your work conditions, your dietary habits, your life experiences, your stresses, various things that you go through, can all have damaging effects on your sperm's health. You will probably never notice it with the naked eye, but health of sperm does vary with time.

These days a lot of men try to set some financial or career goals first, or they are influenced by their friends' ideas of a life free of responsibility, or they just want to enjoy their youth while it lasts. But that all vanishes when their friends start settling down. Then they get serious and try to get into a stable relationship. Financially it may make sense to wait, but you may be causing yourself a potential headache for future baby planning due to your aging body parts. For you, being, say, thirty-five is like being a young and most eligible bachelor. But in fact, half of your self manageable life is done and your time is running out to have a natural healthy pregnancy. Not trying to scare anyone but please wake up!

Basically once you go into adulthood, your body starts ticking. So if possible, the sooner the better. Try not to wait for decades. Living for the moment might make you happy for a couple of years, but for the betterment of your long-term family plans, having a solid vision of the future might make you happier and more confident as you grow old.

CHAPTER 5

The Planning

LET'S TALK ABOUT THE ACTUAL planning for your body and mind to be well prepared for the day of conception and beyond.

Let me summarize it for you in just four simple steps:

- Enough exercise
- Good hygiene
- Good food habits
- Spending family time

1. EXERCISE

Our bodies are nothing but delicate organic machines. The more you nourish your body, the more benefits it gives back to you. Keeping it healthy for pregnancy planning does not mean trying to get six-packs abs or losing twenty pounds! (Of course, if you think you have gained some extra weight over the years, shedding some may not be a bad idea if you can manage.)

It means, every day for at least a couple of weeks or months before your planned attempt, you have to do enough exercise to keep your blood flowing and get sweaty; basically do something more than your daily routines.

It could be as easy as an hour dedicated to walking or run or other cardio such as a nice long swim, biking, or yoga—whichever method of healthy exercise you are comfortable with. The key is to do it regularly and make sure not to do it too much. Excessive exercise can hurt your body, so keep it balanced.

If you are a regular gym person, plus one health point to you! You are already working toward better health than other people with sedentary lifestyles, those who claim to be too busy, or those stuck on their gadgets.

Needing more time to watch TV or to browse the web cannot be an excuse for not having enough time to exercise! Your e-mails will be in your inbox, infinitely waiting patiently for you. Your TV shows can be recorded and watched later. But now is the time you need to move your body! You can easily exercise for up to an hour a day for a better body, despite how busy you might think you are. Think about a time in a day for your own health improvement, decide and just stick to the plan.

2. GOOD HYGIENE

It is extremely important to keep your basic body hygiene while you are preparing for your big day and even later.

Not washing your hands with soap after using the restroom, or after being around people who are sick, could be a way to get distracted by some illness when what you should be concentrating on is making your body better. *Any illness affects your sperm's health directly.* You can clearly sense it. When you are feeling ill, your body automatically stops urging for anything related to sex.

Washing your hands with soap a couple of times a day, especially every time you use the restroom and every time you come home from work, is the best way to start. Washing your hands before and after you eat instead of just using a napkin is also important.

I recently watched a TED Talk on "The simple power of hand-washing"—a must watch. The speaker, Myriam Sidibe, has her PhD in washing hands with soap—the topic is that important! If you really want to be surprised, just observe your restroom visits and see how many other people wash their hands with soap. It feels like some people just don't believe in soap. Please be cautious and wash your hands with soap.

You might laugh off the idea of skipping daily baths, but I have seen people do it, especially on weekends when they are just being lazy. I was one of those people during my college time, but thankfully not anymore. Please don't do that.

Keeping your private areas cleaner, especially before (and after) you are going for some bed action, is also important.

In general, any sicknesses is what you should try to avoid so that your body will be better prepared. A lot of people might think this is a long stretch, but every simple improvement adds up to better health and eventually to a better and stronger you and your sperm.

Why risk anything when we can avoid unnecessary illnesses so easily? Plus keeping yourself away from illness means not spreading any illness to your partner—who along with you is also preparing her body for pregnancy. Remember once you both start planning for pregnancy, you no longer are two separate individuals with their own spaces. You will find taking care of each other more. You both are part of the same equation now.

3. GOOD FOOD HABITS

We usually think that better food planning is for a new mother to worry about. We let them eat all good foods while we men, on the other hand, enjoy eating whatever we want to.

You are what you eat after all, and the same goes for your sperm. It's not only women's turf to worry about food for pregnancy. Having better food habits will take you a long way. (I have also added a full chapter called "Food: For Her" that you might find useful as well.)

Do not stick to the same food items every day. The more varied and nutritional food you eat, the better it is for you. If you are a salad eater, try mixed greens instead of just lettuce as a main ingredient. Having fruit daily will definitely help create quality liquid for sperm to swim in. If you are a meat eater, I would suggest avoiding eating big portions, especially of red meat. Start introducing more greens, fruits, and beans.

I am a vegetarian, many people often ask me, (so cliché) "Where do you get your proteins from?" I ask them back, "Ever thought, where does an elephant get proteins from?"

You will find proteins everywhere, not just in meat!

Enough protein intake is very necessary; be it from meat or greens or beans or lentils, make sure you get your daily protein from somewhere. Avoid artificial protein shakes; you cannot really know the details of all the chemicals in them, or their side effects, so eat more natural food instead.

Real fruit and berry smoothies are the best. Make smoothies your friend; those really help with better and stronger movement of sperm.

If you are looking for some snacks at work, do not open a bag of potato chips and some soda; try some fruit and yogurt.

Get in the habit of eating nuts every day (provided you are not allergic, of course). Nuts have a lot of amino acids that do wonders for your body.

If you can afford to get organic food for a couple of weeks before conceiving, that can help avoid any animal-borne illnesses, GMOs, and pesticides. Make sure you always wash all of your fruits and vegetables.

Please strictly stay away from smoking, regular alcohol intake, any illicit drugs, pesticides, and exposure to heavy metals through food, as far as any in take in body is concerned. There are scientific reports on coffee every now and then; some say it's good, some bad. In general, see if you can limit coffee intake to just a cup or two and not overdo it. Overconsumption may kill your appetite for food and may reduce your metabolism.

And, just because you are getting very enthusiastic about baby planning, *do not* start taking her prenatal vitamins—for you—thinking that those will boost your own fertility health as well.

Prenatal vitamins are geared toward improving women's health and preparing her body for pregnancy. Though it's not proven that women's prenatal vitamins are either good or bad for men's fertility health, I would personally avoid using them. But surely you want to make sure she is taking them regularly in proper amounts, on the recommendation of her doctor, of course. Prenatal vitamins are really good for her. One good side benefit of having prenatal vitamins is that she will start looking healthier and better than usual.

If you want to supplement your health along with your regular food, you can take a men's daily vitamin that contains extra vitamin C, vitamin E, folic acid, and zinc, mainly to promote your fertility and potentially reduce some birth defects and some sex health issues.

Remember anything other than food should be used just for supplementing your health. If you are eating a variety of good food daily, anything extra is mostly not needed anyway. Please check with your doctor for anything specific.

4. Spending family time

After a hard day of work and errands, it's very important to spend the rest of your time with your family. Try to stay away from gadgets and spend more time with them, especially your wife.

Your wife will expect more from you—especially the implicit assurance that you are always with her in this big decision and on the journey of parenthood.

Talking about having a baby, discussing plans, and preparing for a new baby will definitely help you create more of a bond with your wife. It will make your wife, and everyone around her, more comfortable with the idea of your new role as parent.

From my personal experience, finding the baby name was the hardest part. After literally discussing baby names for the whole nine months, we settled on one just a couple of days before the due date. So you might want to start discussing that early on. Be passionate about names, but don't argue over them. In fact, it is most likely you will lose any arguments with a pregnant lady! So make your point slow and steady if you are that passionate.

There is another important aspect of spending time with your wife, and that's touch. I will get straight to the point; you will need to be a hugger! Whenever and wherever possible! There, I have said it. It will give you benefits for a long time in your relationship. When talking about baby planning, women get overwhelmed. It's the overexcitement, it's the uncertainty, and it's the insecurity of the future. It's also about the passing of youth, concern about getting back into shape after pregnancy, fear of labor pains, and worry over the baby's health. There are a number of reasons, but all you need to do is give her a nice hug and tell her everything will be all right. Remind her that you will be with her to help her out in all situations. There—you have won half the battle already.

In the world of media, experts say a picture is worth a thousand words; In a relationship I would say *a hug is worth a thousand words*! It will make your relationships with your loved ones last longer. As Mother Teresa used to say, touch heals, touch connects, touch soothes, touch is very important.

Surprisingly, I learned this from my father. He is a person who is extremely dedicated to his work. He was very punctual and was mostly busy working, resulting in less time with us kids. But whenever he had time, he would sit near us. He would ask us what was going in school or tell us how important it was to learn various things at school. Whenever he got time for us, he stayed in close proximity and made physical contact. And for any important events in my life, he always made sure that he was physically present, for us, near us, every single time, however busy he might have been.

Touch—being close or physically present—even if you don't get a lot of time from a person, will create a lifelong bond that unconsciously registers in your mind. It not only makes you feel good, but it also makes you feel more secure and more confident as you grow old. *Life is very simple; more you observe and self-realize, simpler it gets.* Try to think about your own growing up experiences and look for simple things that will most effectively help you with your future parenting.

CHAPTER 6

Choosing the Day

THIS IS THE MOST MISUNDERSTOOD part of a pregnancy. Most of couples think that just having unprotected sex will result in a pregnancy, but they may not be aware that the timing has to be absolutely perfect!

You may feel that you have been taking good care of yourself and you are now ready for some real action. You may get some fun times, but that may not necessarily result in pregnancy. So it's time for you to learn a little more about a woman's body. All right, I can hear what you're saying right now, but please bear with me here. You might learn something new. And this will help you choose a perfect day.

FINDING AND CHOOSING THE DAY

The egg in a woman's body needs to arrive at the proper place in her body, and once it's there, it stays there in its most healthy condition for up to twenty-four *hours* only! How are you going to know when this happens in her monthly cycle? Don't worry, there is help. Thanks to *over-the-counter ovulation kits for women*, it's very easy to test. Yes, there is such a thing!

For the average woman, the egg is ready and in place any time between the tenth day and the eighteenth day, counting from the first day of her last period. All you have to do is test her hormone levels with the ovulation strip and you will know when the egg is present and waiting. Every woman has a different monthly cycle. If it's irregular, chances are the duration of egg readiness will vary too, so it's better to test with a kit rather than leaving it to chance.

Some people may not want to do such tests, and that's perfectly fine too. You can check with your physician for alternatives, or you can keep trying a couple of nights after the tenth day and up to the twentieth day. Doctors say usually sperm can stay alive in a woman's body for three to five days, so you might get lucky and have your sperm in the right place when the egg is ready.

There is a reason why I said you might get lucky—that is, *if* the sperm can stay alive long enough inside a woman's body. Even if you have tens of millions of sperm at your disposal, only one finally gets to enter the egg. Their journey, once inside a woman's body, is more arduous than what *Frodo* experienced in *Lord of the Rings*. There are no shortcuts or help. There surely are companions but it is like each has a ring of its own to care about and a burden to unload. Each sperm is on its own, and it has to travel a great distance, considering its size, to find the egg and meet with it. One single goal to rule them all—the ultimate competition for life and survival! Yes, I am a *LOTR* fan, but that's exactly what I really feel a sperm has to go through, against all the odds. For *LOTR* fans out there, let's not discuss what is *Mordor* here, you did not hear anything from me, let's concentrate only on Frodo and his ring.

Only the healthiest sperm survives this journey. The rest of them rest in peace trying—or worse, get attacked by the female immune system or are simply discarded. This is the reason why we men are given millions of sperms, not just because we can but because the quantity matters for a chance of producing at least one quality sperm that will do it's job flawless. That's why we men need to go through good preparation to improve the health of our sperm. If you do, there's a higher chance of pregnancy when you plan for it (assuming your wife's health is normal).

I hope you are now more clear on why so much importance is given to the health of sperm prior to the pregnancy.

It's better to be the controller of the situation than to be at the mercy of it!

THE PLANNED DAY

On the planned day, before you do anything, make sure the place you have chosen is the one you both are very comfortable with. Some people are not comfortable doing anything in hotel rooms, for example.

Don't worry about what you eat on that day but make sure you both have eaten lightly and are well hydrated an hour or two before the action. A full stomach will make your body concentrate on digestion rather than on your goal, so eat light, and no alcohol whatsoever during that day—or even a couple of days before—for both of you.

Do not think of using any lubricants during intercourse, as any additional chemicals may harm the natural setting for the sperm.

And last but not the least, do not go to bed with stressed minds and bodies. Get enough rest early on, and do not plan any tiring physical activities before or after.

Insisting on not going to bed with a stressed mind has a funny personal background behind it. I tried to follow a very traditional Indian article on what to do on the planned day. I tried to follow every single instruction given about what to eat, exactly when to eat, in how much quantity, special exercises and all the *blahs*, and following that all unconsciously gave me so much stress on that day that when time comes to do it, guess what happened? Nothing! Everything felt so artificial that we decided to call off the plan and got out of the house. We went out to soup plantation to get some nice warm soup, chatted completely on some random topics, went on some night time peaceful beach walk, and when we came home, yes, we did it, and gladly we were done as planned but this time with absolutely no stress.

Now that you both have already decided on which day to do it, be confident and...go for it, man! This is your day! Remember to enjoy the activity; having fun will make your mind and body more accessible and receptive. All the best to you both!

At this point, you are consciously making efforts to get pregnant, so once you are done with chosen day's plan, make sure she lies down for some time. This will reduce the effects of gravity on your sperm who is now trying his best to find and reach his mate.

You will always find friends or people who claim to have knowledge about doing some extra special things to make sure the baby is a boy or a girl, like some magician for gender selection. You can surely listen to them to be respectful, but only for entertainment purposes. It's fun to see how we humans stretch our imaginations in every possible way, but there is nothing medically proven to suggest that there is a definite way to select gender. This world would be a very different place, for better or worse, if such things had worked every single time. So listen, and move on.

CHAPTER 7

The News

YOUR PHYSICAL PART IS DONE. Now you wait for the results. It all depends on how good your and your wife's bodies are prepared for this. Doing all this preparation and planning is all about boosting your chances after all.

If you plan for it, if you keep your bodies healthy, and if you do not have any fertility issues, it is very possible that your wife will get pregnant within a couple of tries—if not on the very first attempt.

It is very important to keep in mind that it's completely OK if your wife does not get pregnant on the very first try. You have to let her know that there is nothing to worry about; sometimes it can take a few attempts.

After trying for more than six months to a year, if there are still no good results, maybe it's time to seek a medical opinion and get you and your wife checked out. It may not be anything bad with your bodies; it's a natural process after all. Sometimes it happens fast, sometimes it can take some time, but if a medical professional identifies an issue, then it's better that you get treated for it sooner rather than later.

If you want a baby, it's better to understand that your biological clock is ticking, so be proactive instead of wasting years of youth.

If pregnancy is not happening even after a lot of tries, and if you are over forty, time is very important. You do not want to waste your time trying things out on your own. You crossed the experimentation bridge long ago. If you are younger than thirty-five, don't panic; nature will take its course in time. You can go on your own for a while and keep trying.

There is no harm or embarrassment in getting yourself tested; you will only help yourself.

Let's come back to the a world where you have done all the right things, and your sperm has found his date. Congratulations! You have accomplished it.

It will take a couple of days for a fertilized egg to set in her body, but most women will know almost for sure when their next period is missed. There are some pregnancy tests that can give an almost accurate result at the first sign of a missed period. It's time to celebrate, but remember, no alcohol for her during the celebration. *Enjoy the news as a couple and as future proud parents.*

CHAPTER 8

Food: For Her

BEFORE WE GO VISIT WHAT *trimesters for men* looks like in next chapter, let's go through some food suggestions for her, because she will keep asking you for it, especially now that she is pregnant.

It's extremely simple and easy to tell a man what to eat and what not to eat and he will do it— very likely—but for some reason pregnant women are not satisfied with these one time suggestions. They are always on the lookout for new foods, and they will keep asking and keep checking for new things. So it's helpful if you have some suggestions readily available for her.

The following is in no way a comprehensive list of food items for her, but these are surely some nice recommendations for you to suggest during or pre/post pregnancy.

Of course, food comes with issues due to the number of allergies and side effects people have these days. So be aware of her food allergies first; you don't want to suggest something wrong by mistake. (Maybe it's a good time to read the book's disclaimer again.)

One quick thing to remember before we dive in: the placenta—the newly grown part that provides all the nutrition to the baby—is an amazing work of nature. It takes exactly what is needed for the baby, in the most accurate amounts and in a timely manner. Anything extra the mother eats will nourish her own body or be stored if it is not useful for the baby at that point in time.

She should not overeat just because she is pregnant. Her body will tell her when to eat.

During my wife's pregnancy, I got very cautious and interested in the food that she ate. I believed that she should eat a variety of foods, in good quantities, at every single meal. But that notion is again simply not 100 percent true. I have seen a few of my wife's friends who, either due to bad nausea or for some other health reasons, did not eat enough or went on a very restrictive diet, and their babies are doing perfectly fine. Again, the amazing work of the placenta. It takes from the mother's body whatever she has to nourish the infant. It's nature's landscape and it knows how to take care of the infant. Like the architect in the movie 'The Matrix Reloaded' says, "There are different levels of survival." So let the new mom decide on when she feels like eating and how much.

Now that we are over the fact that you are *not* going to keep feeding her with your food suggestions or getting possessive about what she eats, let's dive in to explore good food practices for her during her pregnancy.

I am a vegetarian, so even if I research about no-veggie options, they may not turn out good. So I will try to stick to just veggies. I will try my best whenever I'm talking about non-vegetarian meals, but you are free to follow whatever choices you wish to follow.

I have seen some books and many websites that have details about every single nutritional value in a food item, but that kind of information just overwhelms the regular reader, who, like me, is not a nutrition expert. In the real world, hardly anyone measures the amount they eat down to the ounce. They just need to know what to eat and what to avoid.

So let's take a different approach; instead of looking into what each food item has in it, let's look from the point of view of the baby's growth— what food items help the baby grow healthier physically and mentally, and why.

1. IMMUNITY BOOSTERS

The need for vitamin C is hands-down the winner; a lot of foods have vitamin C.

All citrus fruits like lemons, limes, and oranges, and foods such as kale, mangoes, kiwi, and broccoli, have a lot of vitamin C.

Any berries—mix and match, your choice—have vitamin C, as well as a variety of natural antioxidants for better immune support.

2. HEART GROWTH

Berries such as strawberries, blueberries, cranberries, acai, raspberries, and more have super-health powers. They contribute to the growth of many functions. Berries contain folic acid and various organic compounds that help develop the heart and keep the heart clean and disease-free naturally. Folic acid is also very important for her body to produce more red blood cells, especially during the time of pregnancy.

To form various heart tissues, you will need plenty of nutrients such as calcium, phosphorous, thiamine, and copper.

Milk and bananas are very easily available these days everywhere. They contain good amounts of calcium and phosphorous.

Cashews, beans, and oats are known to have needed amounts of copper.

A balanced diet of leafy greens, whole grains, beans, avocados, nuts, proteins, and berries should cover all that is needed for the development of the heart.

Heart development starts from the first trimester. Try to consume less sodium, less cholesterol, and less caffeine.

Extra sodium and saturated fats are especially known to hinder heart growth. Reduce or eliminate the consumption of soda from your wife's diet while she is pregnant.

When it comes to heart and fat for any ages, remember this: Sodium— as in salt—in its most physical nature, has a tendency to deposit. Think of artery blockages. And sodium—as in bicarbonate—has a tendency to bake. Think of obesity.

If you understand this early enough and act by reducing excessive consumption, you might add a few years of healthier life.

Coconut and coconut water in general work magic in a variety of things. Coconut has natural electrolytes, potassium, magnesium, and vitamin C and helps with the extra blood circulation that is needed during pregnancy.

3. BRAIN DEVELOPMENT

A lot of people are very curious about brain development, and so they should be. After all, your and your baby's futures will depend on it.

Brain development happens at a very fast pace while the baby is in the womb. It has to create billions of neural connections, all properly linked and functional. You do not want to hamper the efforts of your genes to make it all happen naturally.

Apart from regular "don'ts" like no smoking, no drinking, and no illicit drug consumption, proper nutrition for the mother is very important for infant brain development. She should eat with that in mind and make sure the baby has what it needs for development. That's why pregnancy preplanning is good for potential mothers, not just for fathers.

Look for foods containing a good amount of omega-3 fatty acids (nuts, organic cheese, soy, flax seeds, seafood, etc.) and folic acid (lentils, beans, peas, dark green vegetables, citrus fruit, Brussels sprouts, fortified cereals, avocados). Folic acid once again takes the crown by contributing to the prevention of a variety of birth defects of your child's brain and spinal cord.

Foods high in vitamin E (leafy greens, seafood, fortified cereals), DHA (seafood, DHA from prenatal supplements), iodine (iodized salt, milk), zinc (poultry and dairy products such as yogurt and cheese) are also healthy.

Seafood in pregnancy is a topic of discussion. It does have a lot of benefits with omega-3 fatty acids and DHA fatty acids, but these days you have to be very careful about mercury levels in seafood. Remember, the bigger the sea fish in size, higher the mercury levels. So if you are a seafood lover, please choose your fish carefully and/or eat it in moderation. Increased mercury levels in your own body can cause harm to brain development in your baby. Any extra dose of heavy metal is bad, even for your adult body. This applies to potential fathers as well during their food preparation.

This is all the "nature" part so far. But on the "nurture" side (though it is not related to food), I would like to mention that brain development is known to flourish when new mother listens to good music, like Mozart, or classical instrumental music, when you sing soothing songs, and read aloud. If you ever planned on learning a music instrument, now is a good time. Learning something new in pregnancy kicks in new creative thoughts and new brain activities in her body that overall helps with better thoughts and feeling of renovation. Try to do regular pregnancy exercise and reduce the stress around you.

4. BONES

What comes to your mind first when you think of bones? Yes, you are right: calcium. Calcium is absolutely a must for building the skeleton, the solid foundation for any physical body. Without strong and properly structured bones, the baby will not be healthy. No one wants to be Mr. Glass from the movie Unbreakable.

But you cannot eat calcium-rich foods alone. Vitamin D plays a big part in making sure the calcium you consume gets absorbed into your body. So what's the most common food source with calcium and vitamin D both that you can find in grocery stores? Milk with vitamin D.

Hey, but what about people with an intolerance for milk? In the world of food, you can always look for an alternative to get the same benefits. Try eating kale for example, it has a very high calcium-absorption rate in the body. A lot of cruciferous leafy greens are also high in vitamins C and K, which are important for keeping bones strong. Also for vitamin D, apart from milk, there are a lot of products that now come with fortified vitamin D, like orange juice and soy or almond milk. Mushrooms such as portabella also contain natural vitamin D.

Now, there is also the most natural and more preferred way to get your daily vitamin D, and that's from early morning gentle sunshine. Apart from a variety of benefits, it also contains the most amount of vitamin D. Along with your regular food habits, a morning walk in the first hour of sunshine will be just as beneficial.

5. PRENATAL VITAMINS

This is not a part of natural foods, but vitamins should be a part of a woman's pre pregnancy planning. These days, hardly anyone gets to eat fully balanced, nutritional meals every time, and if you are working, chances get even slimmer. At least a month or two before she wants to get pregnant, taking prenatal vitamins is super beneficial. You can get them over the counter without any prescriptions. You can check with her doctor for any specific brand and for information on what quantity of ingredients to look for.

Remember you are what you eat. Your baby will get used to what her mother provides to her. If she eats nutritious foods, it will be passed on to her baby. Food is one topic you should not be ignorant about during pregnancy.

Avoiding birth defects and making a child strong for her future is one of the most important things you as a future parent should look out for.

My Favorite Supplemental Food Trio:

Now, a couple of food items from the *land of Ayurveda, India*: Being born and raised in India, I would love to bring my most favorite food trio to your attention: *Turmeric, curry leaves, and mustard seeds*. Indian cooking is heavily inspired from Ayurveda doctrine; it not only tastes good, but if done right it also has a lot of medicinal values that nurture your body and mind. If you find the following information useful, you can definitely try these in your cooking. You will find these items in any Asian grocery store.

Turmeric: Turmeric is nature's wonder food. It has super healing and cleansing powers. In India, people use turmeric powder for a variety of purposes, applying to the skin for any infections, stopping blood from wounds, cooking etc. It is a natural antibiotic and used a lot in daily cooking. Most people all over the world use some form of chocolate in their daily milk. While chocolate is tastier, a lot of Indians also use turmeric in their milk. One forth a spoon of turmeric in a cup of warm milk makes your body naturally detoxified, and it just heals a lot of things in your body automatically without you even knowing it. It also has cancer-fighting properties. You can try putting a few pinches of turmeric or half a teaspoon in the water when you cook pasta, noodles, or rice or when sautéing vegetables, etc. Though it will make your other cooking ingredients look yellow, they will surely taste good as well.

Curry leaves: This is another of my personal favorites. It is usually used as a flavoring agent in India and in many cultures around the world. It will not only give your food a nice aroma and taste, but it will also provide a lot of health benefits. A couple of curry leaves while you sauté your food is more than enough for a day. It controls a lot of digestion problems, and it has a lot of antioxidant, anti-inflammatory, and cancer-fighting properties. It is also known to reduce bad cholesterol levels.

Mustard seeds: These are small seed balls that look totally unattractive but are super healthy in nature. Once you add these to your spice drawer, it will add another dimension to your cooking and health. These are kind of high in calories, so please use sparingly, a pinch of mustard seeds while doing food sauté is more than enough. They also contain a good amount of minerals like copper, zinc, and manganese and are high in essential oils.

Mustard seeds have natural B vitamins and iron to help with blood cell formation.

A Few Easy & Healthy Recipes:

That's a lot of food suggestions, but what if your wife says, *"I am so bored of eating the same things. Can you find me some new recipes?"* All right, here are some nice ones. I want you to be her man in whatever she asks you.

Lentil sprouts: Take a bowl, fill three-quarters of it with lentil raw seeds (toor - yellow lentil (a.k.a. pigeon pea)/masoor-red lentil/mung-green lentil), add room-temperature water, and soak overnight. The next day, remove the water but keep it damp. In another day, you will see nice sprouting action in it. Eat the sprouts cold or warm, raw or cooked, or with some salt. Try them with some lime sprinkled on them. This dish is a nice healthy breakfast alternative.

If your wife is worried about her potential milk supply, throw a few spoonful of fenugreek seeds into your sprouting mix. They will taste a bit bitter, but they work magic in creating milk. This is useful especially after pregnancy. Adding a handful of raw almonds that have been soaked overnight into the mix will also help with her milk supply.

Lentil soup: Take a small bowl of lentils, fill the bowl with water, and cook it in a pressure cooker. Once out of the pressure cooker, add some water, black pepper, half a spoon of turmeric power, salt to taste, half a spoon of shredded garlic, and half a spoon of butter. Serve hot with fresh sprinkled lime juice and garnish with freshly cut cilantro. Yum…

For all chicken-soup lovers, I would like to invite you to give lentil soup a try.

FreshenUp drink: (At least that's what I called it when I marketed it to my wife.) This simple, easy-to-make, nutritious drink is mostly helpful for easing morning sickness and nausea during the first trimester. Heat a cup of water so that it is warm but still easily drinkable. Add half a teaspoon of freshly shredded ginger (or shredded ginger–squeezed juice), half a teaspoon of freshly squeezed lime juice, and two teaspoons of honey. Mix it up and serve, any time of the day; it will freshen her up.

On the topic of food for her, it's important to remember that as the pregnancy progresses, due to the growing baby inside her tummy, there will be less space available for her own food. Ask her to eat smaller portions throughout the day, rather than regular, full-size meals. Also ask her to consume food that's not causing a lot of gases and heartburn in her body. You will save yourself from a lot of food related complaints.

Now, the finale that will make you a super husband. (Drum roll, please) Let's say she is at a point where she is done with pregnancy and breastfeeding. She is then worried about what to do with her ever-flowing milk supply and how to stop it. Now it's time for you to step in with a suggestion. Give her some nice *sage* tea a couple of times a day for a few days. Her milk production will just disappear naturally, and who gets the credit? You, my friend! You might just receive the A+ husband grade that you were waiting for, for all your hard work.

Alright, enough of food, lets go through next what *you* will go through during *her* trimesters now that she is surely pregnant.

CHAPTER 9

Trimesters Of Men

By now most men would think, "This is it. My work is done." In a way, yes, you have reached a milestone as a man on your own evolutionary path. But surely your work is far from done. In fact, it is just getting started, and it's more fun if you look at it in a good way.

You always hear about trimesters for women and what they go through, but no one ever discusses what a man goes through, or what a man needs to know for himself during those trimesters.

So here they are, the trimesters of and for men:

First trimester of Men: *The settling of the feeling*

and balancing the delicacy

You can go through potentially three very different phases in this very first trimester. The good, the bad, and—hopefully not—the ugly.

First, there is the excitement of figuring out if she is pregnant and the joy of hearing that news. It's very joyous and very memorable. Treasure this moment, for there is nothing like it.

After a couple of weeks, she will start showing a variety of pregnancy side effects like nausea, mood swings, sudden fatigue, or a special liking or disliking toward some foods. If you are a first-timer to the pregnancy thing, you will start thinking, "What's going on? Did I miss some memo? Isn't this supposed to be a happy journey?" But you have to understand that this is not her; it's the new hormonal changes that her body is trying to adjust to. So be patient. Be with her, and don't get angry or frustrated because of any physical or behavioral changes. She is not going crazy—she is not doing it intentionally. In fact, she does not even know she is doing it, so just try to relax and react normally to her needs. Be helpful.

In my case, my wife just could not handle the smell of sautéed food. She would feel very nauseated, and sometimes she just started crying for no good reason. Offering my help with some of her cooking in her first trimester helped.

You have to keep your cool and be with your wife whenever she needs you. Being with your wife does not always mean that you have to be physically close to her. Most of the day, most of us will be working somewhere outside of the home. It's not possible to cater to every single need and emotion of your wife immediately. But these days most of us are connected through technology. So when you have free time, you can always have a small talk with her over the line.

If your wife has a good support system from her family and friends, then your load will definitely be lighter, and that's good for you. But if you are the only one who is with her now, then she will keep needing more attention from you. That's natural, especially in times like these.

The last (ugly) phase is something that hopefully no one has to face, and most people do not, but it's important to know it regardless. (If you happen to be a pregnant woman in normal health reading this book, you may want to just skip this part and go to the second trimester of men.) I only dare to write about this along with the topic of the joy of hearing the news because we men—or rather the non pregnant, non hormonal partner—can digest difficult situations more gracefully and are better at being prepared for anything. Yes, I am talking about losing the pregnancy, or a miscarriage.

The first trimester is very delicate in terms of her body settling into new changes. Sometimes, depending on various external situations or physical conditions, a pregnancy can go wrong. During this difficult time, it's extremely important to be with her.

Along with her, you have to give yourself some time to heal from this loss. Find ways to help yourself adjust to this situation. You will have to first discuss it as a couple. Please don't blame her. Try to understand why it happened and if there was any way it could have been avoided.

You can also get support from family and friends. I understand that telling this news to anyone is a big deal. People can go through a lot of things, worrying what other people might think, but letting this news out and getting support from other people is going to help you regardless.

One thing I have observed over and over is that spreading the personal sad news decreases the sadness in you. And, especially when your sad news does not involve a financial burden for other people, people are usually very willing to help with mental support. The more you talk about it, the more you will hear people's views about it. The bad feeling eventually decreases, and with time you will start building your confidence back.

So let your friends know, at least the close ones. It helps you move on faster. As time passes by, you both can definitely recover from it. Things will change and you will be ready once again to embrace the parenthood that you are waiting for.

Miscarriage is definitely not the end of your happy story. Even though there is a little bit more risk in future pregnancies, medical science has become so advance now that with proper medicines and with proper nurturing, any future miscarriages can be avoided. So try to move on with the past and embrace the able future. (If you wish to read more on miscarriage, there are variety of resources on internet and many published books on it, one quick read I would recommend is from babycenter.com search for 'Understanding miscarriage'.)

In my case, my wife experienced blood suddenly oozing during her first trimester, so we rushed to the emergency room. As you know, the emergency room in the United States is not really an emergency room. They make you wait for a couple of hours regardless. But after doctors checked her out, everything was all right. It was probably just some sudden bodily movement that caused it, but the baby was just fine. In fact, that was the day we heard the baby's heartbeat for the first time. We went through a variety of emotions before the doctors got time to check her. A difficult time in the pregnancy could be as straightforward as this. In any case, you both need to be with each other, making each other comfortable and stronger.

SECOND TRIMESTER OF MEN: *THE BABYMOON*

This is really the most awesome time in the whole nine months of pregnancy.

Her body is now settled with the new baby inside her. Risk of miscarriage is almost gone. She has less nausea, and many of the other side effects that affected her in the first trimester are gone. She does not feel as risk averse as in the first trimester, her belly is growing, and more and more blood circulation is happening around *that* area—which in turn could make her *want* you more. Lucky you! All you have to do is surrender yourself to her for any inviting requests. That's why many people call this trimester the babymoon time. You won't be getting anything more than this for many months, so enjoy it while it lasts.

Apart from the babymoon, the second trimester is really refreshing in general. You both are getting ready for parenthood. You are free to share your happiness with the world. You are already talking about baby stuff, feeling the movements of the baby, and talking to the baby; the baby's name is a real issue now; and you get to know the gender of the baby if you choose. It's all fun times.

By the way, it's very hard to say no to the doctor when the doctor asks you if you want to know the gender. We initially decided to keep it a surprise for ourselves, but when the doctor asked, we just could not wait any longer to hear it. Regardless of the gender, you will find yourself smiling and thinking for a long time after finding out.

I am not sure which country you are from, but some countries have a ban on knowing the baby's gender for a variety of social reasons, so please respect the law and act accordingly. It can be fun to keep the surprise until the end.

THIRD TRIMESTER OF MEN : *LOOKING FORWARD*

One feeling that I had during the third trimester is that it is *never ending*, almost. You have already experienced a full six months of pregnancy, and there are three more still to go. These three months feel like they take forever to finish. It surely feels like nature has a dial-up connection to download the full baby. But nonetheless, these three months are extremely important for your baby to survive in the outside world. Do attend to all the concerns and needs of your wife.

Her belly is growing a lot now and there is less space for her own stomach, so tell her to eat small portions through out the day and well before her sleep time otherwise be ready to hear about acidity/heartburn issues at night. Make a better food schedule for her, if she does not have one. Her frequent restroom visits is a very common side effect of third trimester.

Walking is one of the best exercises she can do in this trimester. Remember to take her on long walks, but make sure she doesn't get dehydrated. Our nighttime, hour-long walks and chitchats were some of the finest memories of this trimester for me personally.

At the end of this trimester, her body will start practicing contractions little by little. Tell her to not be afraid; it's very natural.

It is also highly recommended for you both, as a couple, to go and attend a few sessions on delivery-day preparations. Maternity departments in hospitals and/or health insurance companies have some information about those sessions, try to find out by calling them. I personally learned a lot in those classes. Before that, I absolutely had no idea that (spoiler alert ahead) a few minutes after the baby is out of the womb, all of the placenta also comes out. Yikes! But it's good to know such things in advance and not freak out in the delivery room. These classes also teach you both how to do various breathing techniques based on your health conditions, etc. It's very helpful information in general. Try to attend at least one of those sessions, if you can.

Sometime during the middle or end of this trimester, please go visit the hospital that you have chosen. Make an appointment and go see delivery rooms, and especially note where to park your car in an emergency, and where to find a wheelchair.

You are all set for the big (daddy) day!

CHAPTER 10

Meeting the Deadlines

Do NOT BE A HUSBAND who does not know or does not remember your wife's due date clearly or can't recall what month your wife is at in her pregnancy. Ignorance is bliss in many situations, but not this. With her womanly instincts, she will remember every wrong answer of yours for any future reference; you have been warned in advance.

From the time she gets pregnant until the time the baby is two weeks old, you are on a clock and you better set up some alarms to remind you of the most important dates in it, preferably a couple of days in advance. So before we deep dive into final labor day fun, here are the most important deadlines that you will face in her pregnancy.

If you both are consciously making efforts to get pregnant, then knowing her monthly cycle dates are important, at least for a couple of months, so that you can remind her to take a pregnancy test when she misses her period.

Once a pregnancy test comes back positive, ask her to schedule an appointment with her ob-gyn. The happy and kind words from her doctor, and the information that she will provide, will be very helpful. Try to go along with your wife during this first appointment.

Her doctor will also give you the schedule of the appointments until the end of her third trimester. Please make a note of all those in your busy calendar.

Try to be with her at least for her first ultrasound appointment. You will get to see the baby in its earliest form, for the first time. It feels so surreal; it's a moment of wonder, a moment to ponder how nature managed to do this all, a moment to be with your wife during one of the most important and memorable moments of her pregnancy.

I would personally recommend you go with her to all her appointments. In almost every one, you will get to see how your baby is growing. You will learn about her health and find out if there will be any challenges in the future. It's also a nice way to connect with your wife with a new common bond that you will share with her for the rest of your lives.

As I said, it's nice to go to appointments, if possible. If not, a normal pregnant woman is not disabled in any way. She can handle a lot of things on her own.

Deciding on the hospital in the second or early third trimester is the best time. Let your doctor or hospital know early instead of waiting until the end. This is due to the uncertainties around a few weeks of final due date. Due date is just an indication of full term pregnancy. It is possible that a woman can go into early labor before her scheduled due date. Be prepared with her hospital bag a couple of weeks in advance as well.

Once you decide on the hospital, make an appointment and take your wife on a hospital tour so that she will feel comfortable knowing the place. You should know the overall layout. I remember running around the hospital corridors in the middle of the night to find a vending machine to get some orange juice for my wife.

A hospital representative might ask you to come prepared with documents for early admission. Be prepared so that you do not need to get distracted by paperwork on the main day.

Around the middle or end of the third trimester, let your employer know that your wife's due date has come near, that you might have to rush to the hospital, and that you will be unavailable for a few days or a couple of weeks without much notice.

If you are not going to get much help from your family members after the baby has arrived, then I would recommend taking off the first two weeks of paternity leave from your work. You can take more paternity leaves if you like but the first two weeks are very important for your wife's and your child's health. Please check your state's law, you are most likely entitled to a few weeks off of work as part of your paternity leave.

After the first two days in the hospital, my daughter was diagnosed with jaundice, which is not uncommon; we had to rush to another hospital to get the ultraviolet light treatment for one extra night. Sometimes it takes a few days for the baby's health to settle down, so please take at least a few days off.

Within the first two weeks, you also have to find a pediatrician for your baby and take him or her for the very first doctor's visit to make sure everything is fine with the baby and to get a schedule of baby's next appointments.

The first two weeks are about the most basic survival of the baby in the outside world and recovery for your wife, so try to be useful and be attentive to their needs. This is in short asking you to be a superman, which you eventually become by that time!

Alright, hopefully deadlines are all set in your calendar, time to deep dive into *the* labor day…

CHAPTER 11

The Big (Mommy/Daddy) Day

PHEW, ANOTHER BIG MILESTONE IS about to be over. You are meeting all your deadlines on time, and the whole nine months—and especially the last, never-ending trimester—is now ending for real. But the reason the last trimester gives you so much time is to help you relax and to prepare you for the future rush.

You will soon be facing one of the most important days of your life; you have to be well prepared for that.

Some women start getting proper contractions, some will go into labor much quicker, and some will have their water break early. It's different and unique for each woman and its not possible to guess what your wife might go through when her labor day will arrive. It might all look like the start of some chaotic situation, but at this point you are more than prepared for it, and you cannot lose your cool now. Act accordingly based on the specific situation for your wife.

Have her doctor's number, a twenty-four-hour nurse line contact number, and your hospital's maternity department number ready in your own *fully charged* phone in case you need guidance from anyone in these very last minutes. Be in touch with one or two of your close friends or family if you happen to need some urgent help with anything.

It usually starts with contractions that come and go. Then they will come in increasing frequency and will stay longer and longer. Get some confirmation from her doctor about what frequency and how long of a contraction should be considered a trigger to take her to the hospital.

You might think that as soon as she starts getting contractions you will take her to the hospital, but to avoid some unnecessary frustrations and drama on that day it's good to know the hospital's policy. Most hospitals do not admit the patient until some specific length of contractions is reached and she is dilated enough to go into real labor. For hospitals, it's about efficiently delivering the baby and taking care of the new mother when she really needs it, rather than taking care when care is not really needed by hospital professionals. So it's better to know the hospital's policy in advance to avoid confusion.

It all depends on how your wife is feeling. If she is saying she really needs to go to the hospital, even for a check, you take her there without a delay—and please, *drive safely*. Do not try to drive like you're in the labor scene of a Hollywood movie. Those driving scenes are fun to watch but not to be experienced, especially when a woman in labor is in the next seat. She is more than enough to make you feel like you are in an Oscar winning dramatic situation.

Remember, for any real life-threatening emergencies, there is always 911 (or hopefully something similar, based on your country). If you think something is not at all going well with her labor, do not hesitate to call the emergency or hospital numbers.

All right, so you have reached the hospital safely; now what? Find a wheelchair if she is not comfortable walking that time. Take her to the maternity department, which hopefully you have already toured. They will check the status of her labor and will either admit her or wait for some more time (maybe a few more hours) before she is admitted.

Once she is admitted, hospitals usually allow one or a couple of people inside the delivery room with her, so decide—*well in advance*—who is going to be with your wife inside the room. Some men can be very sensitive about seeing blood and the ordeal of delivery in general, so you have to come with a prepared mind. If you really think you cannot handle it, then please get someone close to her, like her mother or her best friend, or maybe even a professional doula if needed. But it is very nice if you are the one to be with her during this time. And, please don't start filming everything because you are very excited. First get a consent of your wife and go ahead only if she is ok. Please avoid any arguments in the delivery room. She is going to have super powers that day, please don't test them.

You might get lucky that your wife could go into final labor and give birth in an hour or two. But you might be surprised to know that many women can stay in labor for many hours. She could be in the delivery room for a long time, and so you better have some food for yourself, as she may not be allowed to eat anything until the final delivery once admitted to the hospital.

Once admitted to the delivery room, discuss all medical decisions with the doctors and your wife, but you have to help keep her morale high and try to keep boosting her confidence to help her get through this painful time with a bit of ease.

Your wife might ask for, or your doctor might suggest, pain medication if your wife is not able to handle the pain. It's her decision to either take it or not. There are some risks involved, so do some research well before the due date so you both are ready with her decision. The same is true for the choice between a normal delivery or C-section; let your wife and doctor decide in case of any emergency. It might be your baby in her tummy, but *it's her body*, and it's the doctor's first responsibility to make the best decisions for the patient's and the baby's health.

My wife got admitted to the hospital at six in the morning, but we saw the baby at nine at night. The day might test your patience. I cried after seeing the baby. I don't know if it was the extreme joy of seeing her or if it was the sudden release of all that built-up stress after so many hours of seeing my wife in pain or if it was the happiness of seeing that my wife was fine and our baby was in her arms. Maybe it was all those emotions together. It's a very beautiful feeling nonetheless. But mind you in advance, this day does test you.

Ever heard of cord blood?

Some couples arrange some kind of blood storage services for keeping the cord blood safe for many years to come. Cord blood (the blood that stays in the placenta and as part of the umbilical cord after the baby's birth) has a lot of health properties, including stem cells, which can be used in the treatment of a variety of diseases. This is mainly used to resolve major issues with the baby's genetic health in the future, especially if you have a family health history of certain diseases. Storing cord blood is totally optional, and it does cost money. Many couples might not opt for it for financial reasons, but now there are many companies for cord blood storage, so check for current pricings. If you do opt in, make sure to let the medical representatives know that your wife is in delivery so they can come and collect the cord blood in the safest way.

POST-DELIVERY: AT THE HOSPITAL

Once the baby is out, doctors and assistants will do all of the work for keeping the baby safe and will move your wife into a regular room where she will be more comfortable to rest. Try to take some rest *if and when* you can.

Doctors and assistants will come and go. They may take the baby out of the room for various medical tests. Insist to be with the baby if they allow. At that age most babies will look very similar, so try to have a good look at your kid. Make note of any birthmarks or physical characteristics. I am not trying to scare you, but try to be with your baby if you can, for as long as you are in the hospital. Our hospital at Kaiser Permanente was nice enough to allow us to stay with the baby all the time, so that was definitely an additional peace of mind.

Make sure to let someone from your work know of the birth so they will know that you won't be coming in for some days or weeks, based on what you have chosen to do. You both will probably be very stressed and tired, so try *not* to call each and every one of your friends with the news. It may be better to announce the good news on some social network so your friends and family know in advance and no one will feel left out.

A pediatrician or two will also visit you guys during your stay in the hospital to perform the first few checkups on the baby. Ask him or her as many questions and concerns you may have.

For any help related to baby feeding for the new mother, most hospitals these days have a support team of lactation consultants, usually free of charge to you. Make use of them for better understanding and to learn some techniques. It helps.

Remember, *breastfeeding is very important*; it is the most natural and healthy food a baby needs. Initially, there can be some difficulties until the baby gets used to it. Maybe you can use infant formula occasionally, but concentrate your efforts on making sure the baby goes back to her natural food supply.

For some reason, if the baby does not get used to her mother's breasts even after a couple of sessions of lactation consultants, you can always let the new mother know that she can pump the milk and give it to the baby in a baby bottle. She might even qualify to get a free pump from your insurance or hospital. Otherwise you can always buy one. You are ready to take your baby home.

CHAPTER 12

Understanding Loss of Balance

From the day you start thinking of having a baby until the day you see your baby, it's very important to understand that it's very easy to lose the balance of life if you do not think it through.

1. Behavioral

From the time you plan to have a baby until you actually have one, it's very important to be in sync with your wife. You both need to be on the same page when a lot of decisions are to be made.

Her mood swings never really go away completely until the very end—it's all those hormones playing around in her body during those months. As you already know by now, she may feel happy and then suddenly some worry will grip her. As a man, it's very hard to understand and explain those behavior changes, and it's easy to get angry or feel frustrated. You have to learn to increase your patience and not lose your cool.

There is also another side effect of pregnancy: her forgetfulness. I don't know what the medical explanation for it is, but I do know from my wife's and her friend's experiences, there is a common chatter between them about how forgetful they were during those months of pregnancy.

For those who cannot handle a lot of confusion in their lives, especially after dealing with a pregnant woman, for your own sanity, it helps if you keep your own exercise schedule. As old and wise people say, *better mind in a better body.* For some peace within, maybe you can try some meditation techniques or even yoga for better concentration and to avoid dealing with small frustrations with arguments.

Try to off-load your pregnancy issues to your friends and family in a lighthearted manner. You will hear so many views, you may even learn from them. Any kind of support really helps.

During your wife's pregnancy, after the first couple of weeks, a lot of things might start irritating you personally. Her list of worries will be unending. At some point you have to do some thinking of your own. Take a step back and instead of telling her not to worry every time, start engaging with her fears. When she sees that you are not telling her to stop worrying anymore but instead are trying to find some solutions for her—not with your own manly, logical mind-set, but along with her—she will start feeling much better.

Don't try to be the most logical and accurate every time, but be reassuring.

If you understand this early on, you will be in a good state of mind and will be able to help your wife more.

2. ABNORMALITY TESTS?

During the course of her pregnancy, there will be a couple of requests from her doctor to test for a variety of abnormalities during the baby's growth. It's pretty much part of their pregnancy-related tests. The Down syndrome test is one of these. Down syndrome is a condition that says the baby's growth may not be as normal as it should be. The risk goes higher for women around forty or older, but for young women below age thirty-five, it's less likely. These tests can be intrusive, so it's always a bit risky. Hearing that your baby can have something like this can cause tension and stress in a family and for a new mother.

But remember, if she is young and healthy, and if your or your partner's family histories do not have any abnormal conditions, then it is less likely that your baby will have any issues. So do your research, seek the doctor's opinion, and then make proper decisions. Just because you have gotten a request to test for abnormalities does not mean your baby has one. There is no need for sudden panic on learning about these tests.

3. Finances

Another thing that might start worrying you is finances. It's very natural to think about finances with a new person being added to your family.

Simple things start getting added to your regular budget:

- Diapers—every month—for the next year or two.
- Baby formula and a variety of specialty solid foods, usually after breastfeeding is over, for another year or so.
- Baby clothes—kids grow out of their clothes very fast.
- Baby car seat—a must if you will be driving with a baby in the car.
- A high chair for feeding—maybe.
- Baby room preparations—crib, room color, toys, etc.

For a baby, there is nothing more awesome than a mother dedicated to giving attention to her baby full-time for the first year or two. But for many couples, both parents are working. After a few months, when her maternity leave is over—and if no family help is available—there will be child-care fees, which may not be cheap.

It may look overwhelming, but these expenses only occur during various phases of your baby's development.

For example, once the baby gets potty trained, then there is no more diaper expense. Once the baby starts going to school, then there are no more child-care expenses (if it's public school, then there are no big school fees as well). Even for nanny expenses, you can look for a tax deduction through child-care credits. Plus with a new family member, you can start getting more tax deductions from your monthly salary. Remember to update your tax forms. This is a savings that you can use for these extra expenses.

If you plan for a baby shower (if your wife is a first-timer for pregnancy, do think seriously of giving her a baby shower to make her feel nice—and if you manage to surprise her, all the better), then make sure to prepare a gift registry of the most essential things that you will need and include it in your invitation. This will help reduce a bit of your own expense.

If you are concerned about finances, you are a responsible person and you are on the right track. This is a good thing. Every little thing helps, so it's not all that bad. Eventually, after a year or two, expenses settle down and do not seem to be that fluctuating.

4. NIGHTLIFE/BEDTIME ACTION? A MYTH?

From the middle of the third trimester until a few months after the pregnancy, you are most likely not going to have any nightlife/bedtime action. For her, during those last months, she is done with all that stuff. She is now having a baby and her body is not even thinking about it—not even remotely—unlike you! So don't even bother asking her to go out or do something special for the night. If you do, this time she will smile and carry on.

Don't feel bad. A few months after delivering the baby, her body and hormones start settling down to normal levels, and you can get back to your regular things.

5. MOVIE TIME?

While the baby is in her tummy, you can go to theaters whenever you want and watch whatever movies you like. There is so much freedom when it's just two of you. So watch as many you want!

Once the baby is out, it might take a (long) while for just the two of you to watch a movie again, especially if it's only the two of you taking care of the baby. Being a regular movie watcher, this was one of the most missed parts of my life for a year and half after the baby was born. Then we started hiring a trusted nanny for a couple of hours every month, and we started going back to the movies.

One nice alternative workaround is to find a play-date for your kid with another friend's kid for a couple of hours. Then you and your wife can go out, have a nice dinner date, or see a movie and have some fun. But please come back to pick your kid up. Don't forget!. Maybe other parents would like to do the same, and you can watch their kids play with yours. Such events not only give you a chance to go out as a couple, which is very important to keep your sanity, but also give kids more socialization.

6. POSTPARTUM DEPRESSION

In some individuals, mostly in women, postpartum depression can occur after childbirth—mostly after the initial enthusiasm and euphoria settles down and the reality of taking care of the baby keeps staring at them, literally. Their baby is going to be with them all the time. There are challenges in taking care of a newborn baby—in addition to newly added responsibilities, the stress that comes from breastfeeding, changes in eating habits for producing milk, worry about losing added body weight, or maybe tensions about rejoining the workforce and leaving their babies in someone else's care—so many things can add to postpartum depression. It's possible to feel a little bit lost and to question various things, but this is a very natural phase. With time it goes away. For some individuals it may not go away easily. Try to be social. Meet with people, share your experiences, read some educational things, and start exercising daily.

The faster you accept the new responsibilities and move on with new activities, the faster you will come out of it. After all, *its just a state of your mind trying to adjust to new realities,* you are not going crazy.

In most cases, it comes naturally and goes away naturally, so don't worry too much. If you find your wife worrying about a lot of things, just try to be with her when she feels she needs you, and be available for any discussions. If you start experiencing increased levels of arguments and behavioral uneasiness between the couple, understanding that one/both of you is going through this temporary postpartum depressions, will make you handle situations more gracefully and in some cases this early understanding might just save your relationship. You might also find a few simple therapy sessions or support/counseling groups useful. But before opting for those, try to give yourself good enough time to realize new adjustments with a new born around you.

7. END OF PATERNITY LEAVE:

Though the first two weeks after baby is born are very tiring, and you are feeling that you need another full week of personal vacation just to relax and unwind, you might be surprised to find some peace in doing regular office work outside the home.

If possible try to get some help for her—a family member coming over to help, or some friends visiting frequently, or some professional helping hand. Or maybe you could offer more frequent massages for her tired body—whichever is possible for you. It's more physically and mentally tiring for her than it is for you.

CHAPTER 13

My Dear Bed: Thou Shalt Not Sleep

YES, YOUR SLEEP SURELY DESERVES a full page even if you have no guarantee of a full night's sleep! Yes, it will be that difficult to sleep for the next couple of (ahem!) years. I am not going to lie; a lot of people will try to console you by telling their current and past experiences. They will tell you that it's just temporary, but believe me, you have to be really lucky to have a baby who sleeps and also lets her parents sleep at least a couple of hours straight! So be prepared in your mind that your sleep will most likely be irregular most of the time.

The first few weeks after the baby is born, the mother will usually get up every few hours to feed the baby, and that might wake you up too. Plus, babies do not wait patiently for their mothers to know when to feed them and take care of them; as soon as they feel any kind of discomfort, they will cry until they are taken care of, day or night—it just does not matter to them.

They are hardwired internally to survive by consuming their mothers' milk whenever their bodies feel the need, and they call for help for any other sanitary needs as well. So for the first few weeks, try to get some rest whenever you can, and whenever you're needed, be a help. If a close family member is there to help you guys, that's a super big relief.

After the first few months, sleep cycles vary per children. Their sleep patterns do not set easily. They go up and down for the first *two* years, and it will most likely be after that that your kid starts developing longer sleep patterns. If she does, good for you! To be honest, my daughter is now over three. She is surely a bundle of joy, but I still feel a bit of hesitation in writing that she sleeps full nights, though it's much better now than earlier for sure. It is kind of scary indeed, but don't worry too much; at one point you just get used to it, and after a year or two passes, your kid starts waking up *less and less* at night. You suddenly start feeling much better, and all things start falling into the right places.

If you are just going with the flow of your free life, totally unaware of what you might go through with a pregnancy, all of above will come to you as a shock. But if you understand it, your mind will be more than prepared to handle the situations as they come, and with proper planning you'll learn to enjoy it rather than getting overwhelmed.

CHAPTER 14

My Dear Parents

Soon one of the greatest milestones in parenthood—pregnancy—will be over, and your baby will be in your arms. You will be proud parents, and that child will be your creation, your genes, your blood in a new and better body. It gives new meaning to having your heart walking outside your body. The satisfaction and achievement of something greater than yourself will stay with you forever. It's time to take a deep breath and take the next steps of parenthood.

I won't soothe you by saying parenting is an easy task in comparison to pregnancy. It is not. If I look back, dealing with pregnancy is rather an easy task compared to the challenges of raising a newborn. But if you have the right attitude and mind-set, it's definitely not as difficult as it may seem.

Like everything in life—your education, finding a job, struggles in a job, the ups and downs of finances, and the challenges of personal relationships and social lives—parenthood also comes in tides of high and low responsibilities.

There are a lot of people who try to avoid having a baby because they think parenting is too difficult or they think they cannot handle a baby. Of course one cannot know everyone's personal thoughts about life, but if you look at it, parenting is just one more thing to handle in life, and like anything else in life, there is nothing to be afraid of.

How many of you think finding a job is an easy thing? Even if you have the proper education, you have to prepare for an interview for the specific position you are looking for. You have to go through job applications, interviews, anticipation, and rejections until you finally get through. The satisfaction of getting a job and starting a new job then leads to the stress of dealing with new responsibilities and moving up in your field. Though it seems like a lot of stress to handle, do you just quit your efforts and do nothing? No, you keep moving forward. Can you get everything on a silver platter by just sitting in one place? No.

To earn anything in life—a job, respect, financial goals, social status, better friendships and relationships—you have to work toward it. Nothing comes easy or for free. *There is no free lunch*!

Pregnancy and parenthood are no different, and fortunately they come naturally, so there is nothing to be afraid of. You have the abilities to handle life's stresses regardless. Parenting is not going to make or break you. Like everything else, it will have its own challenges, and you will have to handle them the best you can.

There is a silver lining with raising a child: you get to learn so many new things about life, and mostly you get to learn more about yourself—which most of us stop doing due to our super busy lives. You learn to make relationships stronger. I personally feel so much more connected with my wife after we had our daughter. My wife who kind of hated the idea of cooking every day before having kid, now takes so much interest in cooking to bring variety in my daughter's diet and has become an awesome cook. For me, who totally hated the idea of keeping house clean every day, now helps my wife with special *clean up time* that we do with our kid before we all go to bed. These are very small things in third person's perspective, but many small things like these bring a better kind of peace in a relationship. As time goes, parenting makes you better at handling all other responsibilities. You may not even notice that parenting taught you so many things.

Apart from life learnings, you get a life long companion that you can call your own, you can depend on, not 'in-law' but genetically bonded with you, who will truly understand you. It takes out the nature induced genetic sadness — that may come with not having a kid as you grow old — out of complex emotional equation of your life. Now a days many people don't think beyond finances when it comes to brining their first kid into this world; But ups and downs of finances come and go many times in one's life, if you have some financial buffer to start with, you can manage it. As I mentioned before positive effects of having a kid outweigh any other possibilities.

I am slightly transitioning into parenting, but at this stage in the book, I think you have gotten enough knowledge about pregnancy and advice on how to deal with it in a positive way. Hopefully your attitude toward pregnancy and approaching parenthood is better than before reading this book. I wish I could write more on parenting, but I will give you some summaries here.

INFANCY AND BEYOND

There will be challenges with the baby's health for the first few months, starting with her food, her growth, and pediatrician appointments. The first few months come with a lot of questions. There are many Internet resources —Wikipedia.com, BabyCenter.com, and WebMD.com, just to name a few— available that deal with newborn baby issues. There are also lots and lots of useful articles and many books on parenting.

Apart from the Internet, the best resources would be your own parents and your friends who have recently gone through a pregnancy and are dealing with a baby. Ask them questions. They may be able to answer most of your questions, but for anything super specific, there are always twenty-four-hour nurse lines and pediatric services that you can get advice from. For any urgent health issues, do not hesitate to call emergency numbers such as 911 (or 112, or 999, or the specific number for your country). Your baby's life and safety should be the utmost priority of your life.

Shortly after the baby is born, you will probably go back to work. After a few weeks on paternity leave, try to prioritize your workload. Things will start settling down soon.

The baby starts becoming independent as the months go by. As long as you take good care of her health, food, and sanitary needs, she will not trouble you as much. That's all a baby needs. Don't disturb your baby's sleep schedule, though; she will do the same with you otherwise. If guests come over to see the baby and the baby is sleeping, please let her continue to sleep. A half-tired baby woken too soon has the ability to stress you out. Please don't test her.

Remember, time flies—literally. Your baby won't be this small for long. Babies grow up very quickly. It's like some switch is turned on in their brains, and they start behaving differently with each physical and mental milestone. It's a beautiful and surreal feeling to see them grow. As a responsible parent, you will take care of all of your baby's daily needs. Apart from physical needs, as time passes it is important to nurture them in a positive way. Nature has done its part; now it's on you—both parents—to nurture them and help them not just stay healthy but also become better people as they grow.

In the initial years of babies' lives, there is nothing more than touch and speech that creates the bond between baby and parents. Don't be afraid to take your kid in your arms. The more you hold the baby, the more the bond between you two will grow. Hold her, talk to her, sing to her, read to her. As your baby grows, play with her, get involved in her activities, teach her new things.

At one point, when my daughter was about two, she just refused to sleep. I—being a space science nerd—started telling her the concept of the multi-universe. I don't remember when she fell asleep, but I could not sleep for a couple of hours after thinking about it. But keep telling your child random awesome things, even if she cannot react or speak or interact with you on the same level. She is more than willing to listen. As kids grow, you will be surprised to know how much they remember and how eager they are to learn new things.

The other great effect of raising a kid is that not only do you learn a lot about the *how* and *what* and *what not* of raising a child, but you also learn a lot about yourself too. Many times, parenting will take you back to your own childhood—how you learned things, the games you played, what songs you sang. It all starts coming back and surprises you. A beautiful side effect for me was that I started understanding my parents much better once I started to raise my own child. Realizing all the things they did for you, all the effort, all the sacrifices they made so you would grow into a better person, makes you respect them even more.

Being a good parent, and being available for your family at least a few hours a day, will not only make a strong family but will create lifelong memories and lifelong bonds that you will cherish as your children grow. Please don't keep your family wanting for your time. If you are really busy or out of the house for work, then it's a different story, but try to take time from your busy schedule for your family. It does matter to kids, even if they don't seem to notice or they take you for granted. You being around for them, answering their silly questions, playing with them, teaching them, and getting involved in their lives will make them feel more confident in what they do. Satisfied, confident, and secure feelings stay with them for a lifetime and make them excel.

Like pregnancy preplanning, in parenthood it's also important to prepare and do the right things early on, rather than to deal with negative effects later. That will make your family life happier and less worrisome.

It's almost 2:00 a.m., and it's usually the time my daughter wakes up, calls me, and asks me to be near her while she sleeps again, I will have to go now. As a first-time writer, my book never feels complete and editing seems endless, but I have to stop on a good point, but you keep doing your best. Remember nature with nurture, prepare well, be there for your wife when she needs you, remember all the important dates, remember good food is important for both of you, and, last but not the least, remember not to lose your balance.

I wish you a very happy and healthy pregnancy and a great parenthood ahead!

Best wishes,
Pratik Patil